# Clothes

# La ropa

lah *roh*-pah

**Illustrated by Clare Beaton**

Ilustraciones de Clare Beaton

BARRON'S

# sweater

# el suéter

ehl *sweh*-tehr

# T-shirt

# la camiseta

lah kah-mee-*seh*-tah

# dress

# el vestido

ehl vehs-*tee*-doh

# pants

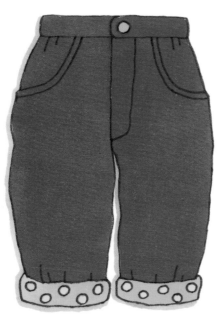

# el pantalón

ehl pahn-tah-*lohn*

# skirt

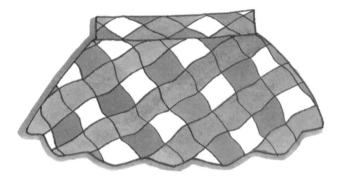

# la falda

lah *fahl*-dah

# shorts

# los pantalones cortos

lohs pahn-tah-*loh*-nehs *kohr*-tohs

# shoes

# los zapatos

lohs sah-*pah*-tohs

# pajamas

# el pijama

ehl pee-*hah*-mah

# hat

# el sombrero

ehl sohm-*breh*-roh

# socks

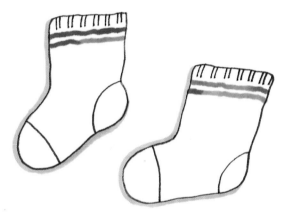

# los calcetines

lohs kahl-seh-*tee*-nehs

# coat

# el abrigo

ehl ah-*bree*-goh

# A simple guide to pronouncing Spanish words

- Read this guide as naturally as possible, as if it were English.
- Put stress on the letters in *italics*, for example, *lohn* in pahn-tah-*lohn*.

| | | |
|---|---|---|
| La ropa | lah *roh*-pah | **Clothes** |
| el suéter | ehl *sweh*-tehr | **sweater** |
| la camiseta | lah kah-mee-*seh*-tah | **T-shirt** |
| el vestido | ehl vehs-*tee*-doh | **dress** |
| el pantalón | ehl pahn-tah-*lohn* | **pants** |
| la falda | lah *fahl*-dah | **skirt** |
| los pantalones cortos | lohs pahn-tah-*loh*-nehs *kohr*-tohs | **shorts** |
| los zapatos | lohs sah-*pah*-tohs | **shoes** |
| el pijama | ehl pee-*hah*-mah | **pajamas** |
| el sombrero | ehl sohm-*breh*-roh | **hat** |
| los calcetines | lohs kahl-seh-*tee*-nehs | **socks** |
| el abrigo | ehl ah-*bree*-goh | **coat** |